The Red-Eyed Tree Frog

Chapter 4
Lesson 59: Many Jobs of Y
Lexile® Measure: 570L

Printed in the United States of America

Copyright © September 2012 by Reading Horizons

No part of this publication may be reproduced, stored in a retrieval system, or transmitted in any form or by any means, electronic, mechanical, photocopying, recording, or otherwise, without the prior permission of the copyright owner.

ISBN 978-1-62382-024-4

You may say that all frogs are green with black eyes. That is a myth. There is one type of frog that has a style of its own. It is a red-eyed tree frog.

Do not try to find this frog in your back yard. Do not try to find this frog in a dry place. This frog lives in the rain forest.

It is green. But it has bright, red eyes and red toes. It blends in well with leaves on trees.

You might not spy these small frogs even if you are standing right by one!

The red-eyed tree frog can stick to branches. You will not see one fly from a tree. The key is the small cups on its toes. The cups are so strong!

It is hard to pry a red-eyed tree frog off of the tree.

This shy frog does not stray a long way from its tree.

It sleeps on green leaves in the day. It stays up at night to play and eat.

A nice meal for the red-eyed tree frog is a big, fat fly. Yum!

Other animals try to eat the red-eyed tree frog. But they are so shocked by its big, red eyes and red toes that they stay away.

If you have not seen a red-eyed tree frog yet, look for one in a pet store. They are great!

The End

Comprehension Questions

1. This passage is about a frog that
    a. can fly.
    b. sleeps at night.
    c. lives in the rainforest.

2. How does the red-eyed tree frog stay in trees?
    a. It does not stay in trees.
    b. A nest helps it to stay in the tree.
    c. With small cups on its toes that stick to the branch.

3. What is a *myth*?
    a. Something that is definitely true.
    b. A creature that lives with unicorns.
    c. Something that most people believe is true even though it may not be true.

4. Would you be likely to find a red-eyed tree frog in a mud puddle on your street?

    a. Yes

    b. No

5. Which person in the following might seem *shocked*?

    a. a sleeping baby

    b. a man who just won a million dollars

    c. a boy watching a movie he has seen 13 times

Skill Words

by*	myth	stay	way*
day*	play	stays	yard
dry	pry	stray	yet
fly	say*	style	you*
key	shy	try	yum
may	spy	type	

Most Common Words

a	great	right	will
all	has	say*	with
and	have	see	you
are	if	small	your
at	in	so	
back	is	that	
but	it	the	
by*	lives	there	
can	long	these	
day*	look	they	
do	not	this	
does	of	to	
find	one	up	
for	other	way*	
from	place	well	

Challenge Words

animals	forest
away	hard
branches	own
even	store
eyed	yard
eyes	

*both Skill Word and Most Common Word